MERCER
ILLUSTRATED

MERCER
ILLUSTRATED

The Places, People, and Experiences of a Uniquely Impactful University

Mercer University Press, Macon, Georgia

MUP/ H1047
© 2024 by Mercer University Press
Published by Mercer University Press
1501 Mercer University Drive
Macon, Georgia 31207

All rights reserved.

This book may not be reproduced in whole or in part,
including illustrations, in any form (beyond that copying permitted
by Sections 107 and 108 of the U.S. Copyright Law and except by reviewers
for the public press), without written permission from the publisher.
© All photographs and images are the property of Mercer University
and may not be reproduced without permission.

28 27 26 25 24   5 4 3 2 1

Books published by Mercer University Press are printed on acid-free paper
that meets the requirements of the American National Standard for
Information Sciences—Permanence of Paper for Printed Library Materials.

Larry D. Brumley, Managing Editor
Matthew R. Smith, Creative Editor
Jan Horne Crocker, Photography Curator
Gordon Johnston, Text
Burt&Burt, Design

ISBN 978-0-88146-938-7
Cataloging-in-Publication Data is available from the Library of Congress

JACKET ART
*Front, the iconic Godsey Administration Building, completed in 1874 shortly after
Mercer moved to Macon from Penfield, was added to the National Register
of Historic Places in 1971; Back, Jesse Mercer Plaza, Cecil B. Day Campus, Atlanta*

The text is set in Minion Pro Display and Meta Sans.
Printed and bound in Canada.

CONTENTS

Foreword by the President • vii

Campuses
MACON • 1
ATLANTA • 41
SAVANNAH • 67
COLUMBUS • 75

LIFE AT MERCER • 83

MERCER IN THE WORLD • 155

ALUMNI IN THE WORLD • 171

Photographers • 187

FOREWORD BY THE PRESIDENT

Founded by Baptists nearly two centuries ago, Mercer University took root in a fertile tradition born out of protest and a commitment to honoring our God-given dignity, protecting our inviolable freedom, and engaging in just and compassionate service. Remaining committed to these founding values, Mercer has equipped generations of students with the skills and knowledge to lead full and successful lives, to empower them to become leaders in communities throughout the world, and to inspire them to deploy their talents to positively impact the human condition.

Mercer today stands among the leading private research universities in the nation. This standing among our nation's finest universities has been achieved without sacrificing our values—without losing our institutional soul. We have preserved a personal and intimate educational experience, while creating a vibrant and caring academic community of innovators, fearless and eager to take on the most pressing challenges facing humankind.

This folio of photographs is intended to capture the values and energy of this very special University. I hope these images of the places, people, and experiences that generate Mercer's strong, humane, affirmative spirit encourage you about our future as much as they do me.

William D. Underwood

MACON
CAMPUS

The distinctive brick spires of Mercer's oldest and most deeply rooted campus have been a Central Georgia landmark since Mercer University moved to Macon from Penfield in 1871. In the century and a half since, Macon and Mercer have grown together into the educational, medical, cultural, and commercial hub of Central Georgia. From one building housing the College of Liberal Arts and Sciences, the Macon Campus has grown to include the School of Medicine, the School of Engineering, the Tift College of Education, the Stetson-Hatcher School of Business, the Townsend School of Music, and (on its own downtown campus) the Walter F. George School of Law, along with programs of the College of Professional Advancement and the College of Health Professions.

The campus breathes in motivated, aspiring students from all over the world, circulates them through challenging classrooms, labs, cultural events, and field experiences (as close as Macon's Pleasant Hill neighborhood and as far away as Botswana and Vietnam), then breathes out graduates who lead, educate, advocate, invent, legislate, heal, minister, perform, and create all over the nation and across borders. Generations of Mercerians have put their educations and edifications to meaningful work, bolstered by the spouses, friends, mentors, and memories they found on the Macon Campus.

Many return to rub again the bronze head of Jesse Mercer that gave them luck through final exams, to cheer on one Bears team or another, to enjoy a performance, to visit a favorite professor, to stroll the quad or Cruz Plaza. To return to green spaces where you can feel the spirit of the community that shaped you and where you can also see that vital shaping continuing uninterrupted for those who have come after you is a personal joy. It's also a way of belonging—a kinship.

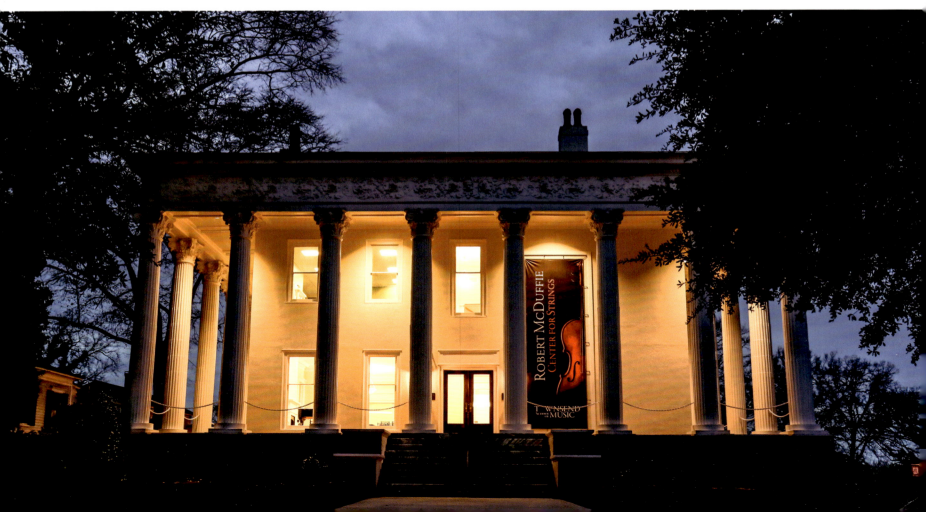

Opposite page, clockwise from top left: Historic Quad, Hardman Fine Arts Hall, The Bell House

Looking out from Hardman Hall

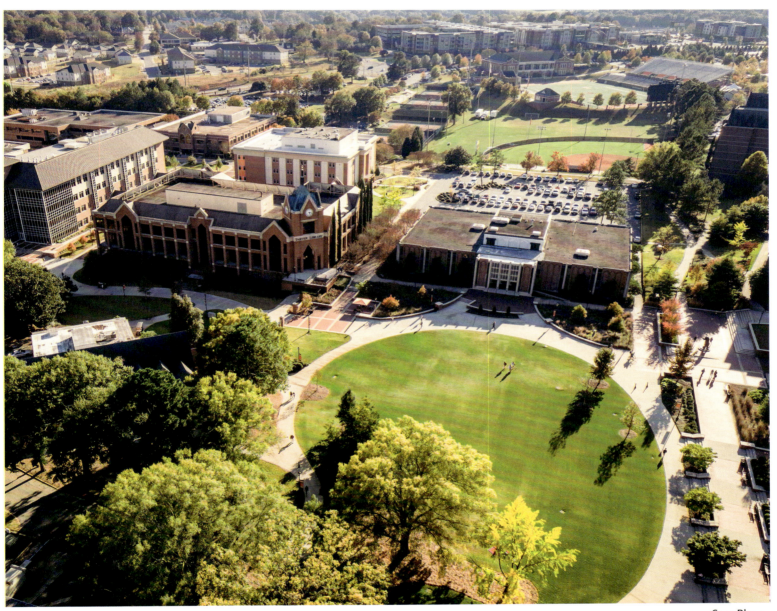

Cruz Plaza

Jesse Mercer Plaza

Willingham Hall

Bill of Rights Eagle in Freedom Plaza

College Street Plaza

Newton Hall

Newton Chapel

Newton Plaza

Opposite: Portico, Mercer University School of Law;
the Spires of Mercer; Mercer University Drive Entrance

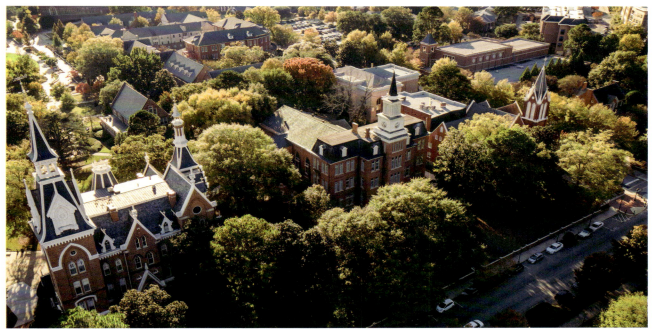

Tattnall Square Park Fountain

Tattnall Square Center for the Arts

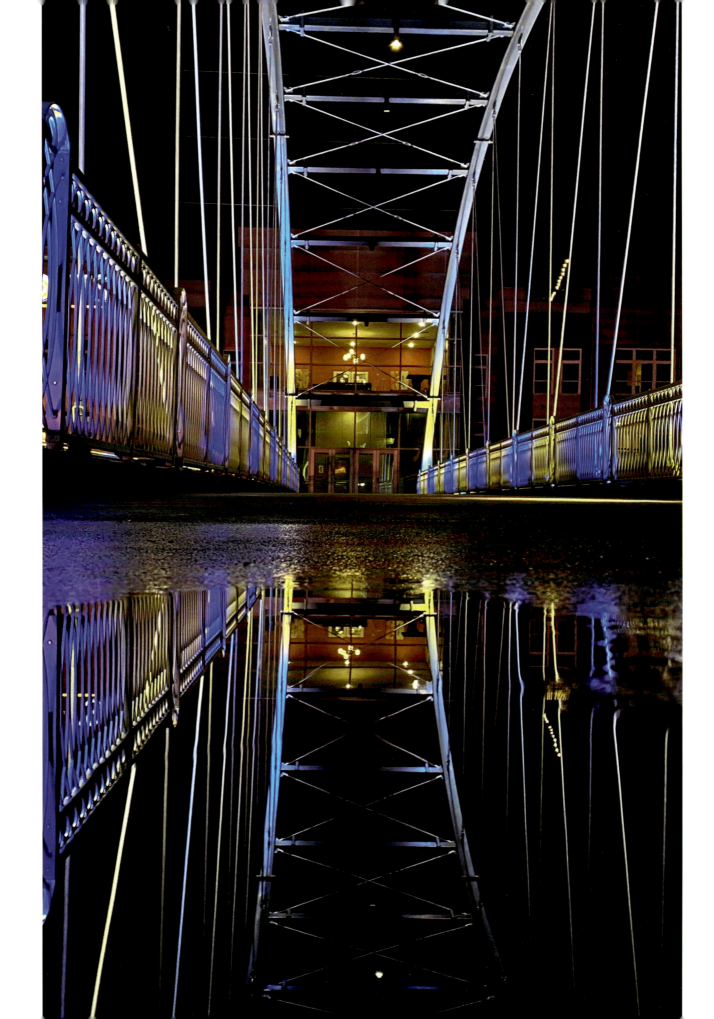

Tift College Senior Bell

Opposite page: Pedestrian Bridge, Mercer Landing

Interior of The Grand Opera House

Opposite page: School of Medicine and A. V. Elliott Science and Innovation Quadrangle

Spearman C. Godsey Science Center

Butler Family Plaza, Tony and Nancy Moye Athletic Complex

Wiggs Hall

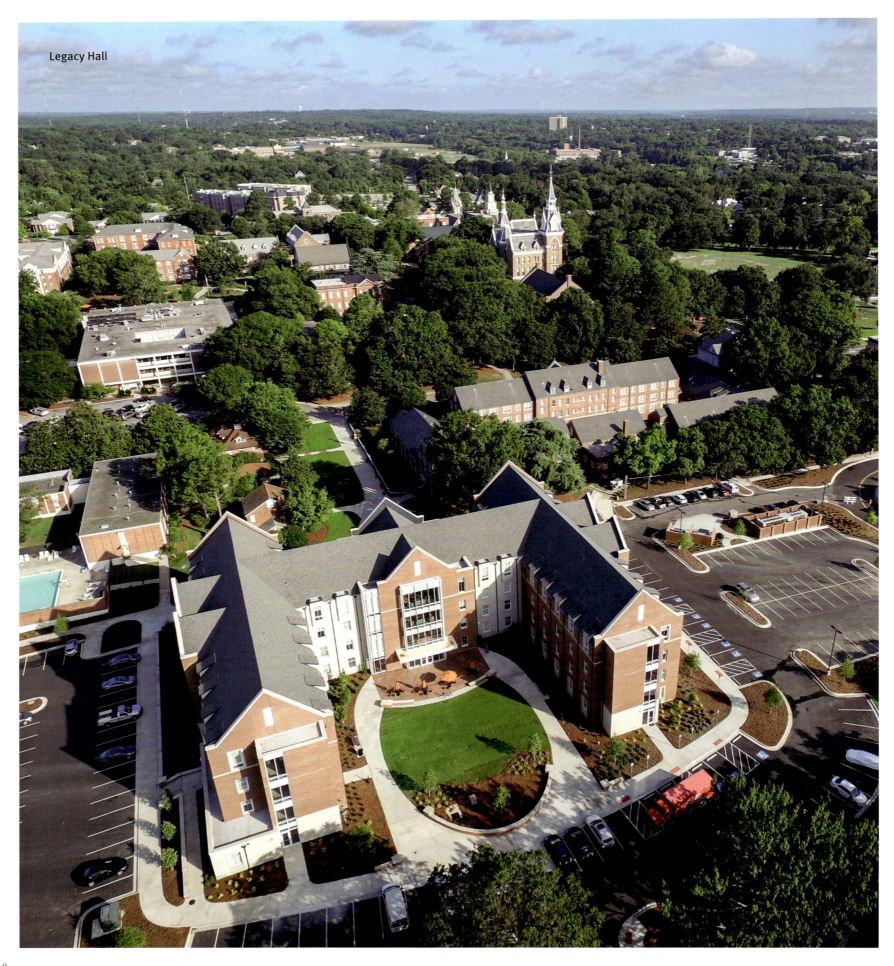
Legacy Hall

Ryals Hall

Mercer University School of Law, Coleman Hill

M. Diane Owens Garden

McCorkle Music Building

Mercer Landing Pedestrian Bridge and Five Star Stadium

Woodruff House, Coleman Hill

George B. Connell Student Center

Downtown Macon

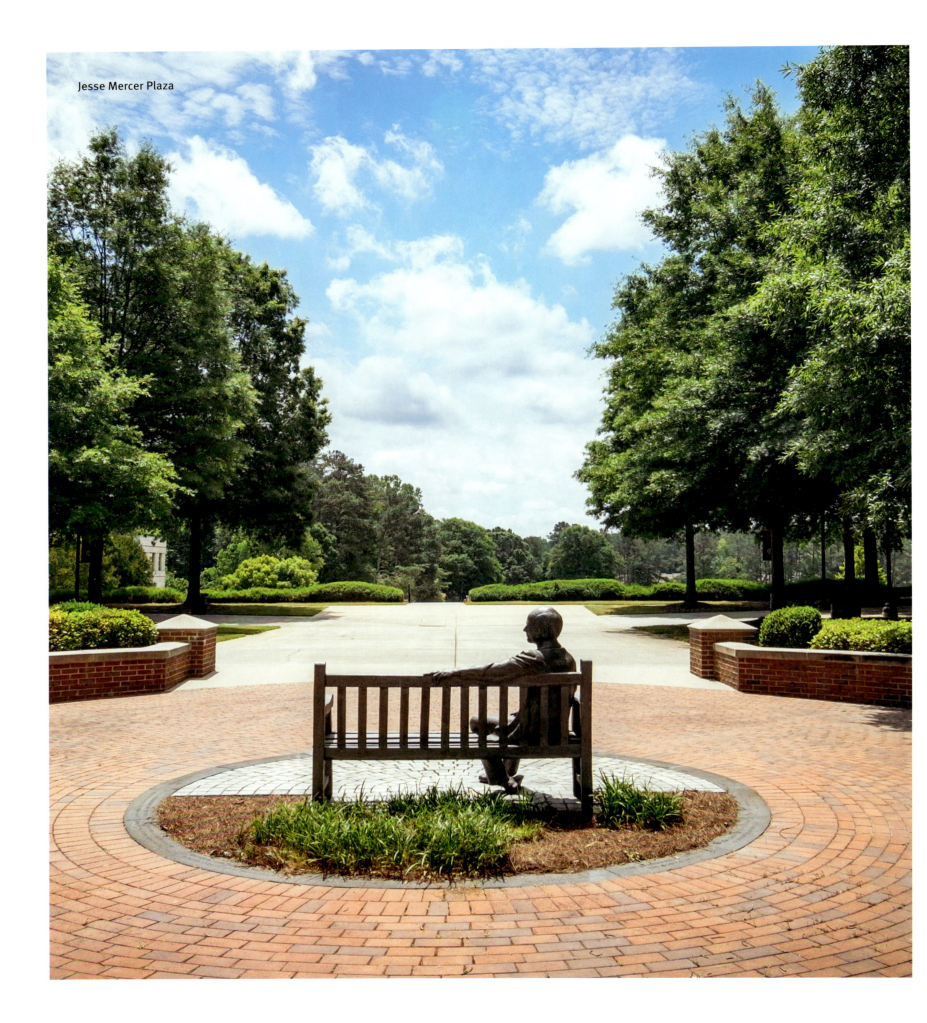
Jesse Mercer Plaza

ATLANTA
CAMPUS

Since 1972, Mercer's Atlanta Campus has been a wooded oasis in a humming, dynamic metropolitan area rich with cultural and arts events, economic opportunity and commerce, and intercultural diversity. The Cecil B. Day Graduate and Professional Campus is home to the College of Pharmacy, College of Health Professions, McAfee School of Theology, Georgia Baptist College of Nursing, and College of Professional Advancement, along with programs of the Stetson-Hatcher School of Business and Tift College of Education. The heart of these 200 acres is Jesse Mercer Plaza, where a statue of the University's namesake imparts a sense of calm concentration and serves as a soulful reminder of the campus's roots, which reach back through Macon to Mercer's original campus in Penfield.

The great distinctiveness of the Atlanta Campus is the variety of focus in its programs and student body—graduate and undergraduate students study nursing, marriage and family counseling, ministry, spiritual formation, business, and teaching, among other subjects, in fifteen different buildings, crossing paths often as they share lunch at Toby's, do research at Swilley Library, work out their bodies at Sheffield Gym, and tend their spirits in the interfaith prayer garden and labyrinth. The state of-the-art Moye Pharmacy and Health Sciences Center, the new home of a pharmacy program that began more than a century ago, like Mercer's other Atlanta-based programs, leavens classroom education with real-world training and experiential learning. Each Atlanta-based program has its own active village life thriving in places like the Moye Center's student lounge, in the Sheffield Center, in the weekly chapel service at McAfee, and in the quiet common areas of the Administration and Conference Center.

Campus Entrance, Mercer Village

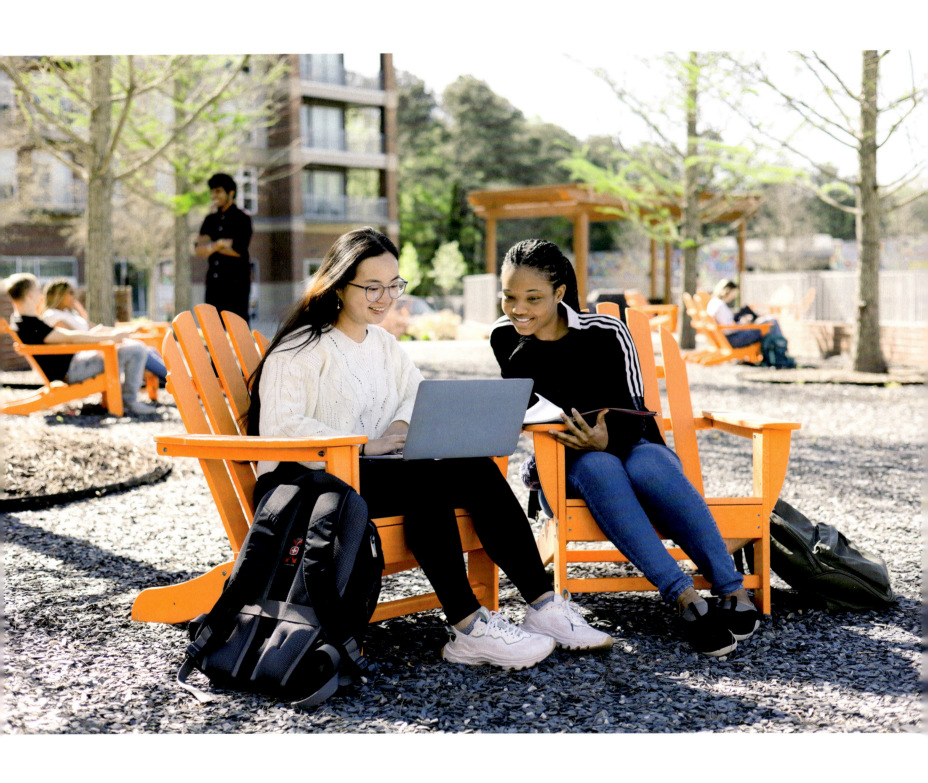

Opposite page: Tony and Nancy Moye Pharmacy and Health Sciences Center

Opposite page: Tony and Nancy Moye Pharmacy and Health Sciences Center

Administration and Conference Center

Opposite page: Monroe F. Swilley Library

Tony and Nancy Moye Pharmacy and Health Sciences Center

Monroe F. Swilley Library

SAVANNAH
CAMPUS

Since its beginnings in 1982, the Mercer School of Medicine has trained vitally needed doctors whose practices save and improve lives. Establishing a clinical relationship with Memorial Health in Savannah in 1996, the School of Medicine's presence in the oldest city in Georgia has thrived, growing into a full four-year M.D. program in 2008. It's hard to imagine a more heartening architecture for a medical education facility than the light-filled atrium at the Hoskins Center in this coastal city of culture, live oaks dripping with Spanish moss, and twenty-two historic squares.

The depth of Savannah's history memorably frames and complements the School of Medicine's state-of-the-art, forward-looking teaching of medical professionals. It seems an especially appropriate place to continue the School's long tradition of improving Georgians' health. More than 60 percent of graduates currently practice in the state of Georgia; of those, more than 80 percent are practicing in rural or medically underserved areas of the state.

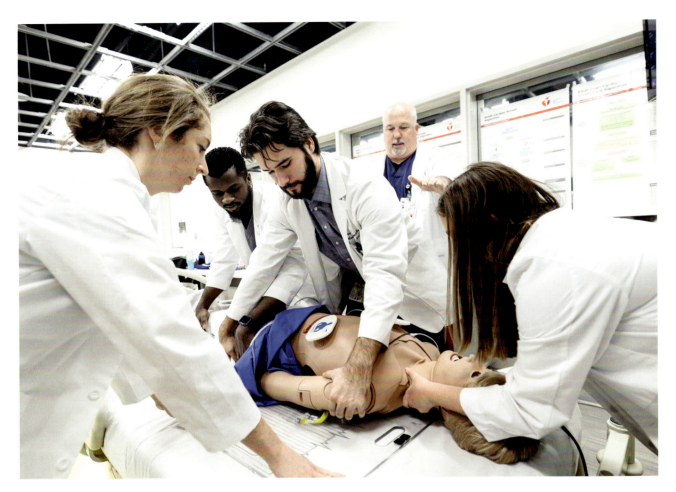

COLUMBUS
CAMPUS

Of all Mercer's classroom and laboratory spaces on its campuses throughout Georgia, none offers a more stirring view than the sweeping vista on the Chattahoochee River visible from the School of Medicine's facility in downtown Columbus, completed in December 2021. On the six-acre site in this bend of the historic waterway, the School of Medicine has increased the Columbus Campus' enrollment and is on its way to a full complement of 240 Doctor of Medicine students, equaling the M.D enrollments in Macon and Savannah. The classrooms, medical library, gross anatomy lab, simulation center, research lab, and vivarium in this sparkling facility make it a health care hub in southwest Georgia, supplying medical professionals to an area of Georgia that badly needs them.

This is the culmination of an effort begun in 2012, when Mercer started offering clinical education to third- and fourth-year medical students in Columbus, establishing the University's third medical school campus in partnership with Midtown Medical Center (now Piedmont Columbus Regional Hospital) and St. Francis-Emory Healthcare. The new facility is connected to Columbus' vibrant downtown by a beautiful walking and biking path on a river celebrated for its whitewater kayaking and rafting.

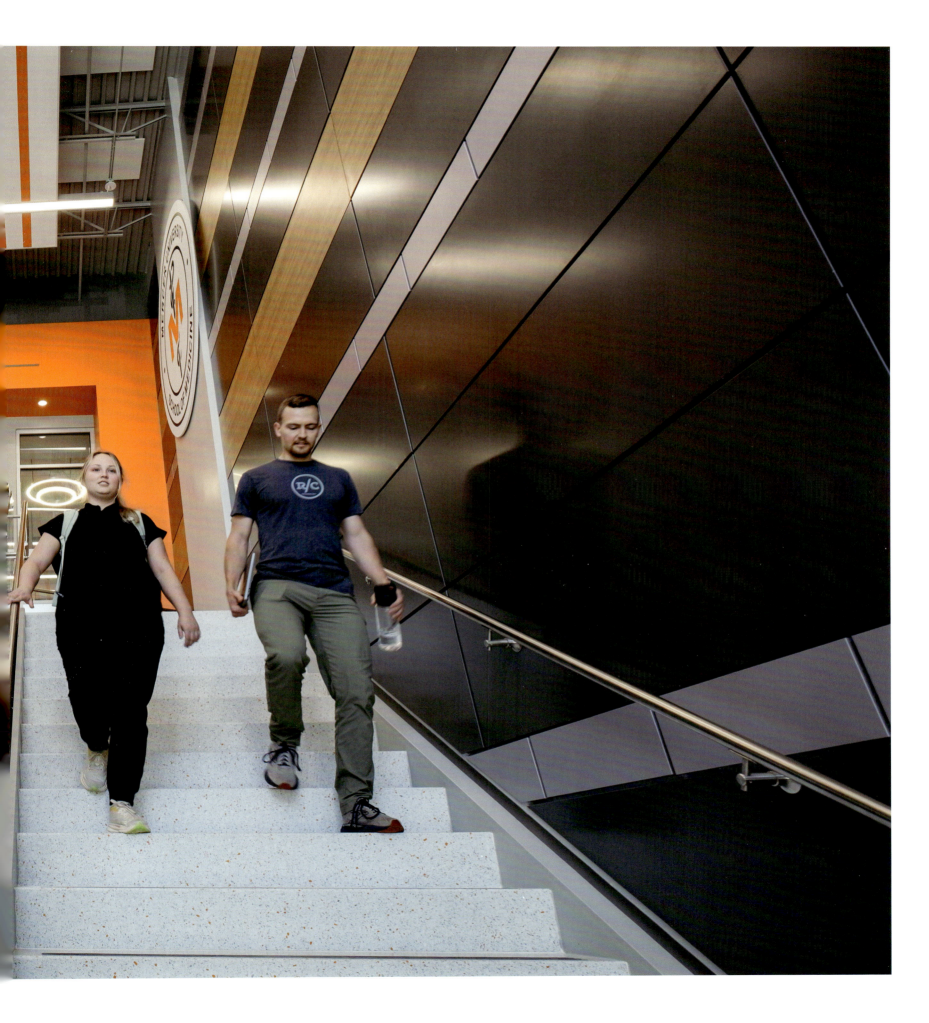

Traditional Freshman Class photo

LIFE
AT MERCER

Education sticks best when it is a communal experience—when classroom learning interweaves with experiences, fellowship, and friendship, when the trials of challenging academic work are eased by the company you keep as you weather them. As Mercerians have gotten smarter together over the years, they have also formed communities oriented around every sort of goal that can be imagined—ending human trafficking, designing and publishing a literary magazine filled with exceptional art and writing, making a community of the corridor between campus and downtown Macon, generating new knowledge through research projects, collecting and transcribing the stories and oral histories of the Pleasant Hill neighborhood and of the Muscogee storytellers at the annual Indigenous Celebration at Ocmulgee Mounds, building a winning soap box derby car, performing a great play, knitting prostheses for breast cancer survivors, restoring a historic park, reading poetry with elementary school students in after school programs, designing a logo to help a local nonprofit fulfill its mission, winning a championship in one intramural sport or another. The list goes on and on.

Some of these communities form around students' wish to do something with the skills and new awareness they develop in classes and labs; others form around the simple pleasure of shared goals and togetherness. The way such communities coalesce on Mercer's campuses is one of its great distinctives. They magnify the surge of Mercer spirit that springs from traditional University events like the annual orange and black reunion that is Homecoming, football and basketball games and other athletic events, Mercer concerts, art show openings, BEAR Day, lectures and symposia, and convocations at the different campuses. Most satisfying of all these events are commencements—that culminating moment when Mercerians take their leave of campus to carry out into the world the abilities and attributes the campus community has cultivated in them.

Mercer Music at Capricorn

Griffin B. Bell and Frank C. Jones Courtroom, Mercer School of Law

103

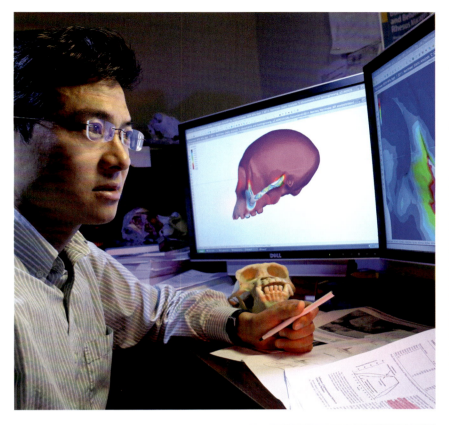

105

107

113

Mercer Theatre

Mercer Singers

Robert McDuffie Center for Strings

Mercer Opera

117

Greek Village

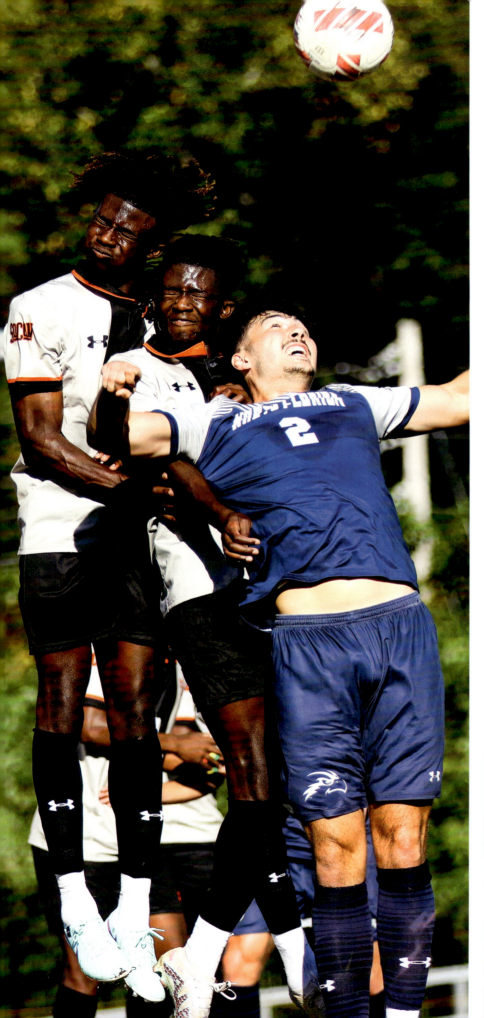

Research Days, Macon and Atlanta Campuses

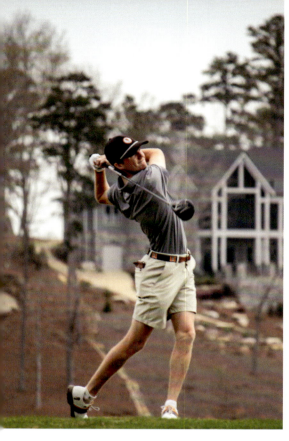

133

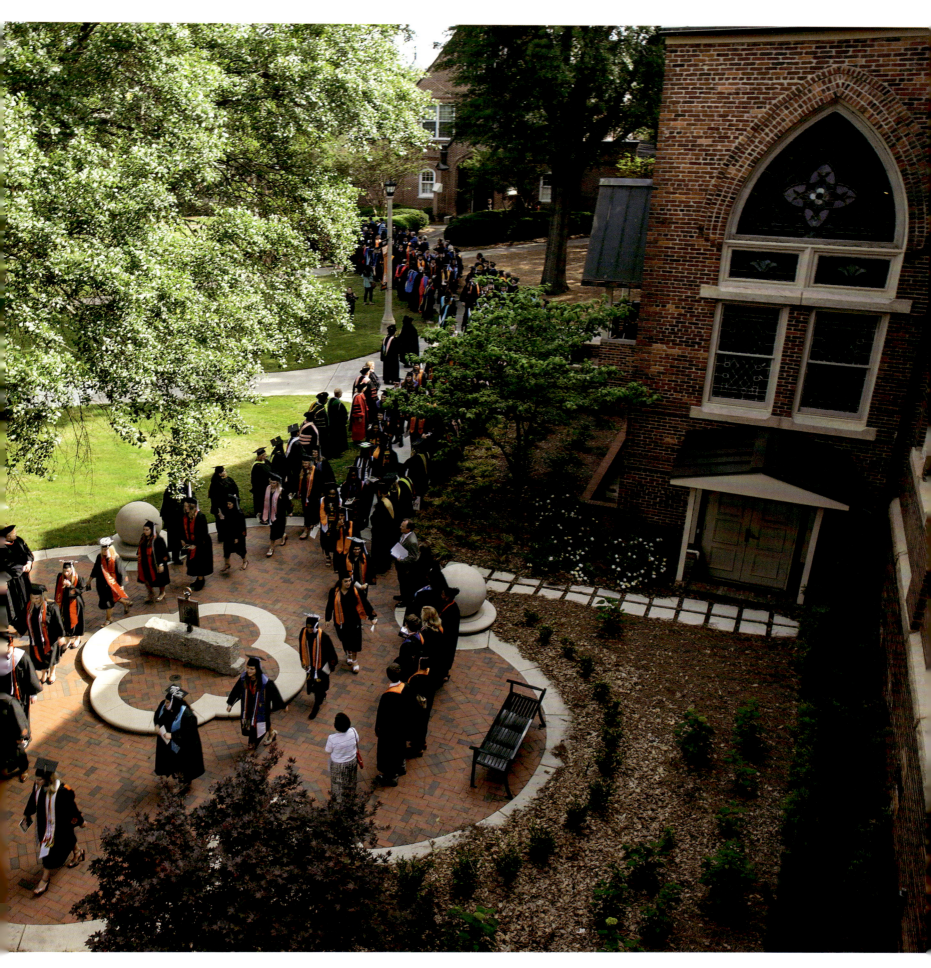

141

Mercer Singers, Neva Fickling Hall, McCorkle Music Building

Mercer plays Carnegie Hall

"A Night of Georgia Music" at The Grand

149

151

Jimmy Carter, Mercer Life Trustee and 39th President of the United States, speaking at the President's Lecture Series in Willingham Hall's Toney Auditorium.

MOM, Mongolia

MERCER IN THE WORLD

Although this folio celebrates the places, spaces, people, and spirit of Mercer's campuses and centers, and although each site is an important point of arrival for the more than 9,000 students who come there seeking education and skills, Mercer is far more important as a point of departure. Since its founding in 1833 in Penfield as Mercer Institute, the University has educated thousands of undergraduate, graduate, professional, and medical students, counting among its alumni twelve governors, twenty-five congressional representatives, a U.S. Attorney General, two Rhodes Scholars, two Pulitzer Prize winners, and many physicians, judges, artists, engineers, scientists, poets, ministers, musicians, educators, business leaders, nurses, pharmacists, and other health care professionals. Even before students graduate, they make forays from the green quads and air-conditioned labs, classrooms, and performance halls of campus out into the world to witness the needs that they will help meet.

Mercer On Mission (MOM) students monitor mercury emissions in gold processing among the miners of Ecuador and Guyana, build water tanks and water delivery systems in the Dominican Republic, and fit amputees with prostheses in Vietnam. In summer 2023 alone almost three hundred Mercer students and faculty worked in fifteen different countries delivering medical care, addressing childhood poverty, designing school curricula, conducting trauma counseling, and cultivating entrepreneurship. Mercer students have held internships at the Carter Center, Georgia Public Broadcasting and other other nonprofit organizations, at businesses, in the studios of well-known comic book artists, and at university presses. Mercer singers and musicians have performed at high schools throughout Georgia and also at Carnegie Hall.

Close-to-home service initiatives like MerServe, Spring Break for Service, Read United, and BearPulse keep Mercerians effectively engaged volunteering and tutoring locally in a way that lets them see how the skills and literacies their studies are cultivating in them can meet immediate needs in their communities. As they master their field, they serve with impact in schools, hospitals, courtrooms, churches, government offices, corporations, and many other places. Even before they complete their major, they are becoming the change they want to see in the world.

MOM, Morocco

MOM, Rwanda

MOM, Morocco

MOM, Belize

MOM, Dominican Republic

MOM, Belize

MOM, South Africa

158

MOM, India

MOM, Dominican Republic

MOM, Dominican Republic

159

MOM, Dominican Republic

MOM, Tanzania

MOM, Dominican Republic

MOM, Dominican Republic

163

MOM, Vietnam

MOM, Cambodia

MOM, India

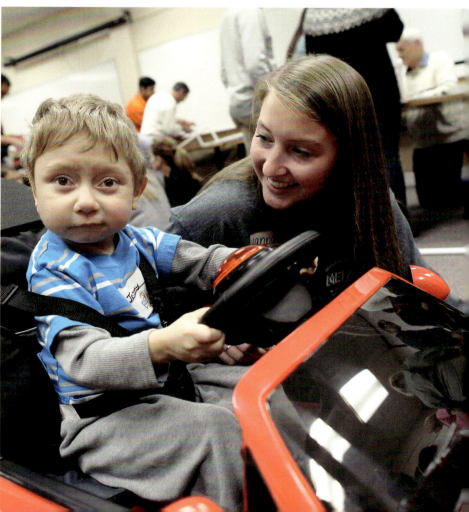

169

ALUMNI
IN THE WORLD

More than ninety thousand Mercer alumni, including alumnae of Tift College, live in all fifty states and in more than ninety countries. They are making important contributions to their communities and their professions. Ultimately, our alumni are the greatest manifestation of the University's mission and its impact on the world. We close out *Mercer Illustrated* with images of graduates representing all twelve of the University's schools and colleges in the settings where they are living out their vocations and avocations.

The ministerial staff of Second Ponce de Leon Baptist Church in Atlanta includes five Mercerians. Left to right: **Rev. Allie Osborne**, MDiv '21, Minister of Missions and Children's Discipleship; **Rev. Dr. Dock Hollingsworth**, BA '84, DMin '08, Senior Pastor; **William J. (Bill) Gabbard**, BA '81, Minister of Music; **Rev. Jonathan Hall**, MDiv '23, Minister of Community and Student Discipleship; and **Rev. John Uldrick**, MDiv '02, Associate Pastor

Amanda Alexander, MDiv '14, Chaplain, Children's Healthcare of Atlanta

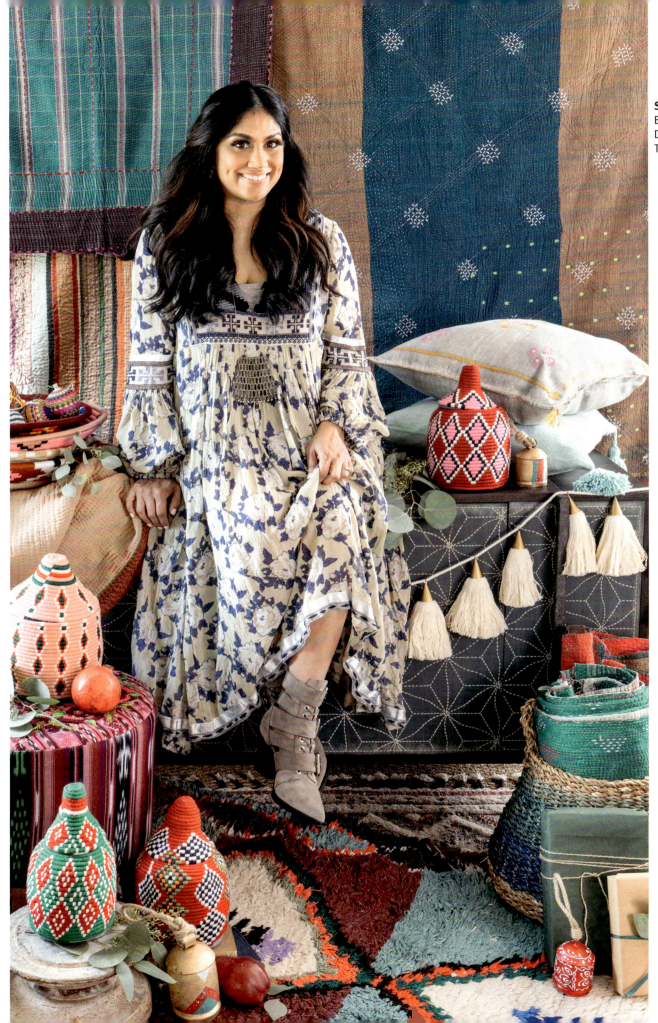

Sonal Patel-Cochran,
BA '02,
Designer and Founder,
Tribe, Atlanta

Clockwise from top left: **Andrew Eck**, BSE '16, Owner, Georgia Artisan, Macon; **Caleb Brown**, BS '16, MS '22, Artist, Atlanta; **Daisha Taylor**, EdS, '23, 5th Grade Teacher and Grade Level Chair, Clayton County Public Schools; and **Keitaro Harada**, BMus '07, MMus '08, Music and Artistic Director, Dayton Philharmonic, Dayton, Ohio

Above: **Nathan Deal**, BA '64, JD '66, 82nd Governor of Georgia, (center) with School of Medicine Nathan Deal Scholars, President William D. Underwood, School of Medicine Dean **Jean Sumner**, MD '86, and Mercer Trustee Terry England; below left: **Stanley Jones**, BS '92, MD '96, Pediatrician, Jesup, Georgia; below right: **Nikki Bryant**, PharmD '03, Owner, Adams Family Pharmacy, Preston, Georgia. Opposite page, clockwise from top left: **Patrice Little**, DNP '18, Founder and CEO, NP Student®, Atlanta; **Hemal Patel**, DPT '18, Physical Therapist, Grady Health, Atlanta; **Thomas Sherrer**, PharmD '13, Owner, Poole's Pharmacy, Marietta; and **Jennifer Tarbutton**, MD '01, Pediatrician, Sandersville

Randy Sides, DPT '17, Physical Therapist, U.S. Army, Loganville

SiHao He, BMus '16,
Shanghai Quartet,
Tianjin Juilliard,
Shanghai, China

Clockwise from top left: **Dominique Michie**, BS '21, UX Designer, General Motors, Douglasville; Macon Leaders, left to right: **Josh Rogers**, BA '05, CEO, NewTown Macon; **Erin Keller**, BA '08, Chief of Staff and Vice President for Development, NewTown Macon; and **Alex Morrison**, BA '07, Executive Director, Macon-Bibb County Urban Development Authority; **Allison Brantley**, BBA '15, MBA '18, Project Manager, TechOps Materials, Delta Air Lines, Fayetteville; and the **Honorable Michael Boggs**, JD '90, Chief Justice, Georgia Supreme Court, Waycross

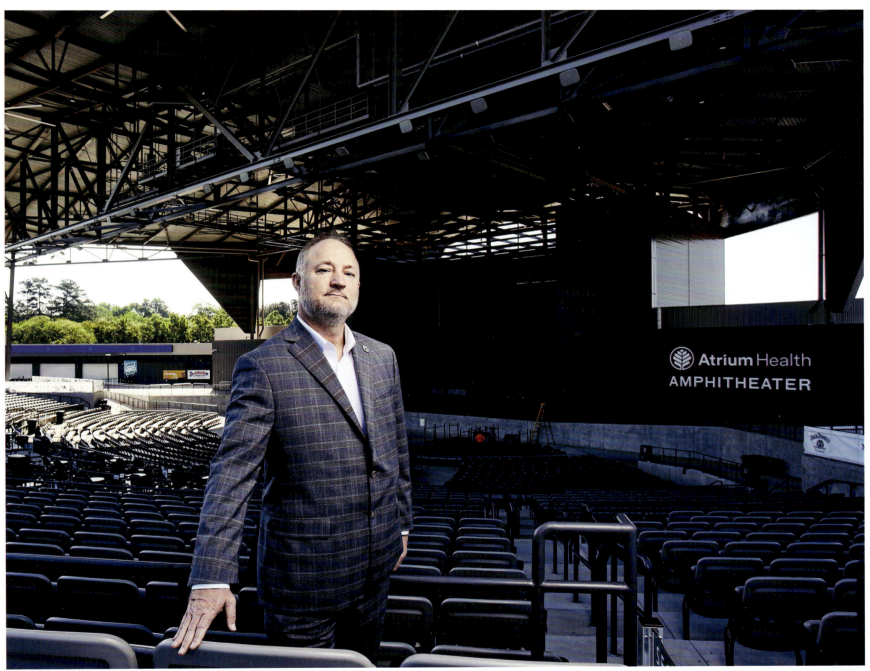

The **Honorable Lester Miller**, BA '91, JD '94, Mayor of Macon

Opposite page, above left: **James DiAngelo**, BSN '07, MSN '11, Executive Director, Nursing Practice and Governance, Piedmont Healthcare, Chamblee

Above middle: Gulfstream Aerospace Savannah Leaders, (left to right) **Johnny Hodges**, BSE '94, Vice President of Engineering; **Naveed Aziz**, BSE '98, MBA '14, Vice President of Completions; and **Vicki Britt**, Senior Vice President, Innovation, Engineering and Flight, and member of Mercer's National Engineering Advisory Board

Above right, Georgia State Senator **John F. Kennedy**, BA '87, JD '90, Senate President *Pro Tempore*, Macon

Opposite page, below left, **Nancy Grace**, BA '81, JD '84, American Legal Commentator, Television Journalist, and Author, Atlanta (left), and the **Honorable Yvette Miller**, BA '77, JD '80, Judge, Georgia Court of Appeals, Atlanta (right)

Below middle, the late **Judge Griffin B. Bell**, LLB '48, 72nd Attorney General of the United States (left), and the late **Robert L. Steed**, BA '58, LLB '61, Partner, King & Spalding (right)

183

Among the many Mercer alumni working at Chick-fil-A's corporate headquarters in Atlanta are (standing, left to right) **Mark Moraitakis**, MBA '96; **Mark Davenport**, BSE '13; **Tunde Ayinla**, BA '17; **Dericus Harvey**, BSE '99; (seated, left to right) **Heather Darden**, BS '98; **Sarah Boyd Pylant**, BBA '18; **Sarah-Anne Crawford Hannah**, BA '17, MAcc '19; **Mary Katherine Savage Laue**, BSE '20; **Lauren Hill**, BS '07; and **Charlie Farr**, BBA '14

Opposite page, clockwise from top left:
Shane Buerster, BBA '18, Owner and Founder, Z Beans Coffee, Macon;
Nancy Bache, BASc '07, Director of Global Talent Acquisition, Acuity Brands, Loganville;
Mac Brydon, BBA '19, Owner and Founder, Bear Food, Matthews, North Carolina; and
Kaitlynn Kressin, BA '15, Owner, Fall Line Brewing, Macon

THE PHOTOGRAPHERS

E very year, more than two dozen talented photographers take thousands of photos for Mercer to help tell the story of this uniquely impactful University. They hail from all over the Southeast, and we are grateful they have contributed their talent, creativity, and perspectives to *Mercer Illustrated*.

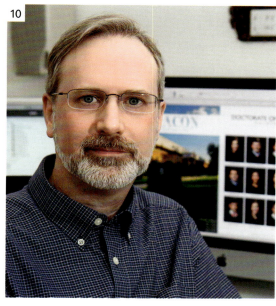

Featured photographers:

(1) **Christopher Ian Smith**, Macon; (2) **Jessica Whitley**, Macon; (3) **Paula Heller**, Atlanta; (4) **Amanda Anderson**, Charlotte, NC; (5) **Matt Odom**, Macon; (6) **Zaina Mahmoud**, Macon; (7) **John Carrington**, Savannah; (8) **Jamie Tucker**, Atlanta; (9) **Matthew Smith**, Macon; (10) **John Knight**, Macon; (11) **Jan Horne Crocker**, Macon; (12) **Billy Howard**, Atlanta; (13) **Marin Guta**, Macon; (14) **Jessica Gratigny**, Macon; (15) **Rebekah Howard**, Social Circle; (16) **Michelle Beavers**, Macon; (17) **Leah Yetter**, Macon

Additional photography provided by:

Action©Hiroyuki, Maryann Bates, Jave Bjorkman, Erin Bowman, Georgia Senate Press Office, Bryant Harden, Turner Howell, Roger Idenden, Jessica Lawhorn, Amy Maddox, Mercer Athletics, DSTO Moore, Mooreshots, Amy Nichols-Belo, Laurie Shock, Stephen Saldivia-Jones, Paprika Southern, and Mike Young

THE DEN

*To learn more about the
people, places, and experiences
that make Mercer uniquely impactful,
visit den.mercer.edu.*